Step-By-Step Guide To Getting Started In The World's Most Addictive Sport: Beginner And Fitness Boxing

The most popular form of exercise in the United States, not surprisingly, is walking and running. The second most popular form of exercise is weight lifting and finally hiking. My guess is if these people had tried boxing before anything else it would be at the top. I've done all three forms of exercise and many others including yoga, basketball, baseball, swimming, and Cross-Fit. If I had to pick one that I could do for the rest of my life it would hands down be boxing. Boxing is addictive. It not just physically addictive it's emotionally addictive as well. What other sport can help build strength, shed pounds, reduce stress, build confidence, allow you to be creative and artistic with your movement, and become more coordinated in the process? Boxing pushes you like no other sport does, boxing holds you accountable in a way no other sport can. If you don't put in the training you won't see the results, you can't fake boxing. If you're not eating well you'll definitely feel it in the boxing gym. The goal of the book is to introduce you to the world of boxing and fitness boxing. If you've already started boxing this book will help improve your boxing skills even further. I hope after you finish reading you'll come to the same realization I've had just how addictive (In a good, life affirming way) boxing is.

The Start

If you're like most people if you don't enjoy doing something you won't likely stick with it. Eventually as life throws curves balls, as you take on new responsibilities, as your willpower fades you eventually give up on well intentioned workout plans. I've been boxing for more than 10 years and still haven't lost my passion for it. Boxing is one of those things that is still the highlight of my day. It feels great from the the boxing movements, to getting out your stress in a constructive way, learning new skills, making new friends, facing new challenges, learning new life lessons, it's a lot of fun. Boxing has so many benefits it keeps you coming back in a way no other sport can compete with. Your workout routine isn't something you dread with boxing it's something you look forward to.

My journey into the world of boxing all started about 12 years ago when I picked up the Tony Horton DVD workout program called P90X. According to Wikipedia, "In 2010, P90X sales dropped off dramatically, however, it still represented half of Beachbody's $430 million revenue in 2010 and had sold over 4.2 million copies (https://en.wikipedia.org/wiki/P90X)." P90X was and continues to be a huge program for the Beachbody company. One of the most enjoyable workouts had to be the martial arts and boxing programs. I've always enjoyed watching boxing and UFC up until that point, but only discovered how enjoyable the sport was when I began doing those P90X exercise routines. On a side note in college I bought two sets of cheap boxing gloves on eBay. My college friends and I used to have all out, no hits to the face, boxing matches in our college dorm room. We didn't know what we were doing so they were always fun and luckily no one got hurt. Well except that one time there was an accidental head butt, but I digress.

Brief History Of Boxing

Boxing as a Olympic sport may have its

origins in the 688 BC ancient Greek Olympic games (https://en.wikipedia.org/wiki/Boxing). There were no rounds and no weight classes so as you would expect heavy weights dominated. "The earliest known depiction of boxing comes from a Sumerian relief in Iraq from the 3rd millennium BCE. Later depictions from the 2nd millennium BC are found in reliefs from the Mesopotamian nations of Assyria and Babylonia, and in Hittite art from Asia Minor. The earliest evidence for fist fighting with any kind of gloves can be found on Minoan Crete (c.1650–1400 BCE), and on Sardinia, if we consider the boxing statues of Prama mountains (c. 2000–1000 BC) (https://en.wikipedia.org/wiki/Boxing)."

Amateur Boxing

Amateur boxing differs from professional boxing in that it's about scoring points and not delivering damage. Amateur Boxing can be found on the college level, in the Olympics, Commonwealth Games and many boxing associations. "Bouts consist of three rounds of three minutes in the Olympic and Commonwealth Games, and three rounds of three minutes in a national ABA (Amateur Boxing Association) bout, each with a one-minute interval between rounds. Competitors wear protective headgear and gloves with a white strip or circle across the knuckle (https://en.wikipedia.org/wiki/Boxing)." Olympic boxing uses 5 judges to determine outcome of a match.

Professional Boxing

Professional Boxing matches go on much longer. The matches range from 10 - 12 rounds for the majority of professional matches (There are some variations depending on boxing clubs and country. In a professional boxing match headgear is not permitted. The fight is stopped if the one fighter cannot defend themselves or is injured. Losing a fight in this manner is called a TKO or Technical Knockout. A fighter has 10 seconds to get back up if knocked down before the fight is stopped by referee. When a fighter cannot get back up or finish the fight after 10 seconds this is called KO or Knock Out. If a boxer is not knocked out the outcome will be decided by 3 judges.

There are many additional rules to Amateur and Professional Boxing, but to the average person the aforementioned are the basics.

Modern Day USA Boxing

The National Boxing Association was formed in 1921. Boxing really took off with Sugar Ray Robinson until his last title win in 1955, then exploded in popularity with Muhammad

Ali, Joe Frazier, and George Foreman in the 1960s and 1970s. During my growing up there was Mike Tyson, and now currently superstars like Manny Pacquiao and Floyd Mayweather. Boxers were kings in years past, but now boxing competes with every other sport on TV. Forget just the UFC you now have NFL, MLB, NBA, MLS, NHL, and WWE just to name a few sports distractions. It's an old argument, but UFC took a lot of boxing fans with them. UFC might be seen by some as a more pure form of combat sports than boxing. I think the attractiveness of the UFC is it solves the age old dilemma if you were in a real street fight who would win? Most likely it wouldn't be the boxer. You would probably need to come from an MMA background with experience in wresting, Jiu Jitsu, kickboxing, and boxing at a minimum. Because boxing limits what you can do, I think it actually makes it that much more interesting. For example take the latest boxing match between Floyd Mayweather and Conor Mcgregor. People wanted to see how Conor Mcgregor would fair when he was limited to using just his arms and boxing skills. I think there is something to be said when you limit one form of martial arts and see who is the best at it. So even though boxing is thought to be on the decline there has still been viewer records broken. Take for example the recent Pay-Per-View broadcasts of Pacquiao, Mayweather, and Mcgregor. People are willing to pay top dollar for the boxing matches that interest them. The matches, though, have to be what people want to see. The boxing contests should be scored fairly and the people putting on these matches have to stay consistent.

If anyone is interested in learning more about the history of boxing there is a great article in the Art Of Manliness blog at ArtOfManliness.com titled, "Boxing: A Manly History of the Sweet Science of Bruising." It's very thorough on the subject of boxing and goes more in depth. Fortunately or may be unfortunately for some this book is not about the history of boxing it's about getting into boxing right now.

Disinterest and Finally Eureka!

I gradually began to lose interest in the P90X exercise programs. There is something that doesn't feel right about working out by yourself and sweating on your brand new carpet with your dog watching. I wanted to be around people, have a real trainer, punch something physical, try boxing out for real. A couple years later a friend of mine heard about this boxing gym downtown that he wanted to try out, he said I should go along. I'm glad I did because that one decision changed the course of my life! From that day forward I was hooked. I had finally found my workout routine and a home away from home. The decision moved me out of your traditional weight lifting and cardio gym to a boxing gym. My friend, unfortunately, lost a weight lifting partner that day. He went for a couple months, but eventually went back to weight lifting.

The Progression

I went to the first boxing gym for about 8 years and bounced around 5 other gyms about 2 - 3 years. I sparred for the first couple years of boxing, but have since only gone for fitness after realizing getting hit in the head is probably not the best idea for long term health. If you are an amateur or professional boxer reading this I have great respect for you. Intellectually you know you are putting yourself in danger by stepping in the ring or sparring with your partner, but there's something so addictive about boxing. As a boxer you know there is danger, but your heart wants to keep on fighting. It feeds your soul, I get why you do it. I will say that in the beginning sparring is one way to speed up your learning of boxing 100x. You will never learn any faster than when you actually have to face real consequences. If you have not been in a fight before someone throwing a punch at your face or body will look totally foreign. When they consequences are real pain your brain works fast to figure out how to avoid the pain that much quicker.

What I Am Not

I'm not a professional boxer, I am still learning, I'm just one of boxing biggest fans. I'm someone that knows a lot about the boxing and especially the fitness boxing world. I've boxed for over 10 years. I've been to six boxing gyms in the USA and one kickboxing gym in Bali where I was introduced to kickboxing for the first time at Daily Gym. If you're ever in Bali be sure to check out Daily Gym, they also have a weight room, very cool spot. From all this experience I generally know what works and what doesn't. I know what a good boxing gym is and what isn't.

How Has Boxing Helped Me?

I used to be a clumsy high school and college recreational weight lifter. I say clumsy because just lifting weights is one of the best ways to get a great looking body that's completely uncoordinated and useless. That's exactly what I was, muscular, but extremely slow and unagile. My body felt like a collection of parts. It makes sense as a weight lifter I would feel that way, that's how you train. For example today I'm going to do biceps and triceps and tomorrow back and legs. Boxing helped connect my body together in one coordinated unit from my feet to my legs up to my hands, it finally could work together again. Yes, I lost some muscle, but I gained a lean body that moves quickly and has more stamina. It built confidence and let me blow off steam when having a stressful day. Going to a boxing gym also let me build a network of friends and acquaintances. Boxing bonds people together. I gained a level of respect for myself I didn't have before that my close friends and family around me could see. Sound like something you want to try? OK, good! Lets get started.

How To Tie Hand Wraps

The first step before any boxing class is putting on your hand wraps. You can either do it when you get to class or before in your car like me. Hand wraps are the first layer of protection before you put on your boxing gloves.

1) First put hand wrap lope around your thumb.

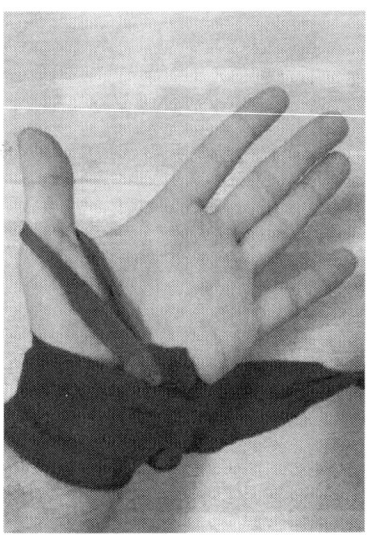

2) Wrap around wrist 2-3 times. There should be tension on the wrap, pulling on the thumb.

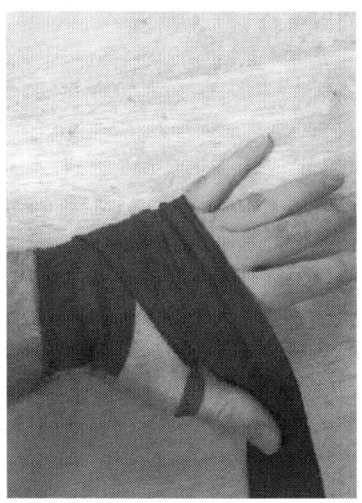

3) Now bring the wrap up from your wrist and start wrapping your knuckles.

4) Move wraps down along the base of the hand and wrap move wraps in between each finder starting from the pointer finger to the pinkie. Be sure to wrap the thumb.

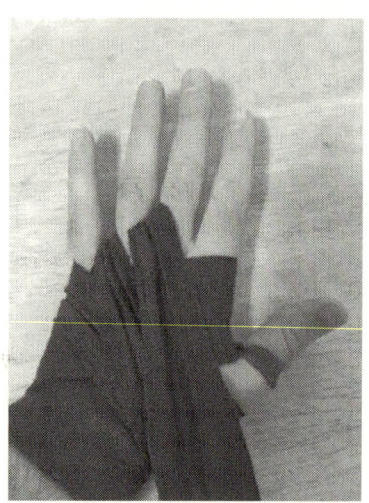

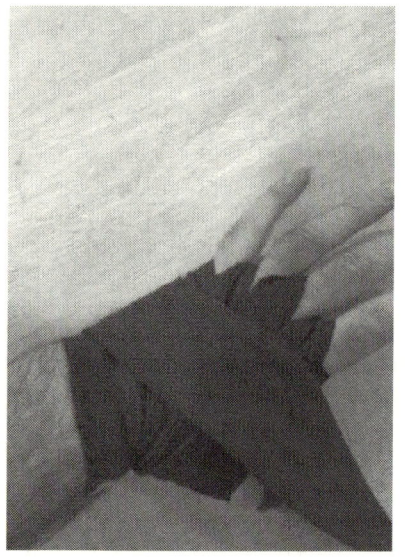

Note: Start moving wraps in between your fingers starting with pinky finger.

5) Once you've covered your fingers move

down to the knuckles and hand. Wrap below thumb and move to wrist as well. Alternate between wrapping the hand and wrist, below thumb.

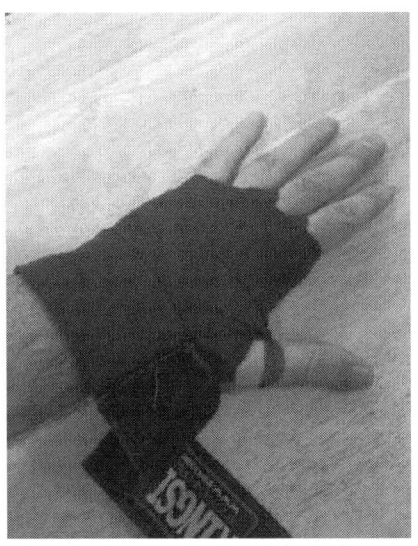

6) Finish wrapping hands 2-4 times around the wrist and Velcro closed.

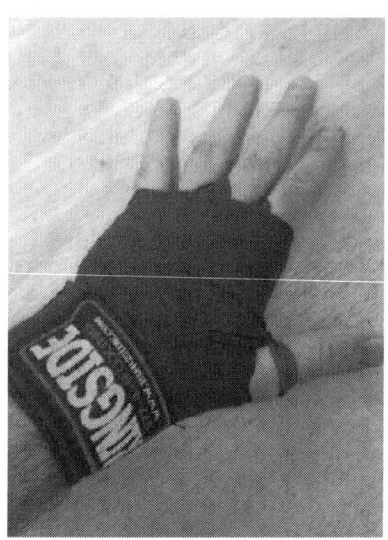

8) Congratulations you are finished wrapping your hands! Repeat process on the other hand. Once you get good at wrapping your hands and commit this to memory it should take less than 3 minutes.

Pictures only go so far. This process is difficult to explain without a detailed arrowed diagram, ask your coach if you are still having trouble wrapping your hands. Coaches are happy to help and it's expected that you don't know how to wrap your hands when you first start boxing. I'd suggest searching online or going to YouTube and getting more detailed information regarding wraps. One good site I found can be found here: https://www.expertboxing.com/boxing-basics/how-to-box/how-to-wrap-your-hands. I just want to give you the basics. The most important thing is wrapping in between fingers for more protection, also protecting the knuckles, thumbs, and protecting the wrists. Make sure your wraps are long enough to accomplish all this.

I've noticed a lot of wraps sold online are not the highest quality. The material I use almost feels like thick cloth. It does not feel like gauze. I'm not sure if there are knockoffs out there, but in my experience a lot of the hand wraps are complete garbage. I used to buy Amber brand wraps at my old gym, they were very thick and supportive. I went online and bought the same brand, but they were totally different. The online wraps felt like wearing light cotton gauze on my hands, they didn't last the first washing, not at all the same. My go to wraps right now are the 'Ringside Mexican-Style Boxing Handwrap, Black, 180-Inch' on Amazon. If you want guaranteed quality I'd say buy them at your gym if they provide wraps or go to TitleBoxing.com. Don't spend more than $15 for wraps. They should be around $10 for a pair.

Quick Hand Wrap Tip

When you're done with wraps at the gym instead of just pulling them off and putting them back into your gym bag try rolling them around your fingers as you take them off. When you're done rolling the wraps onto your fingers just slide them off and you'll have a nice little hand wrap ball free of tangles. Next time you use them they won't be all tangled, wraps will also lay flat. After a while hand wraps can start looking more like rope and not like flat stripes of material as they should if you're not careful. Some gyms will provide hand wrap rollers which can come in handy sometimes if you need perfectly rolled hand warps after you're done boxing. Doing this extends the life of the hand wraps and ensures tangle free wraps next time you dig them out of your gym bag. About every week or so throw them in the laundry and wash/dry as you would normal clothing.

Picking Boxing Shoes

The cheap and easy way I've been able to find "boxing" shoes and this was a tip from an actual boxing couch is to use wresting shoes. Boxing shoes and wresting shoes seem to be pretty similar. I first started with Nike Wrestling shoes, then switched to ASICS Wrestling Shoes, but now have started to shop one of my favorite boxing sites, TitleBoxing.com. At the Title Boxing web site I purchased my current favorite shoe called Fighting Sports Aggressor Mid Boxing Shoe on sale currently for $19.99 retail price is $49.99. This is proof that you don't have to spend a lot of money to get a decent pair of boxing shoes. Getting a good pair of shoes helped my footwork and my feet felt a lot better after workouts.

Quick Boxing Shoe Tip

Are your boxing shoes starting to smell? Lucky for you many boxing shoes are made mostly out of a washable material, not leather. Just throw them in the wash and they'll come out smelling a lot cleaner than before.

Gym Bag Selection

When picking a gym bag I recommend getting one made of cotton/canvas. Pick a bag that you can put in the wash. If you're like me you'll be throwing your boxing gloves, dirty hand wraps, and maybe the occasional workout shirt. You'll want something you can just throw into the wash and clean completely.

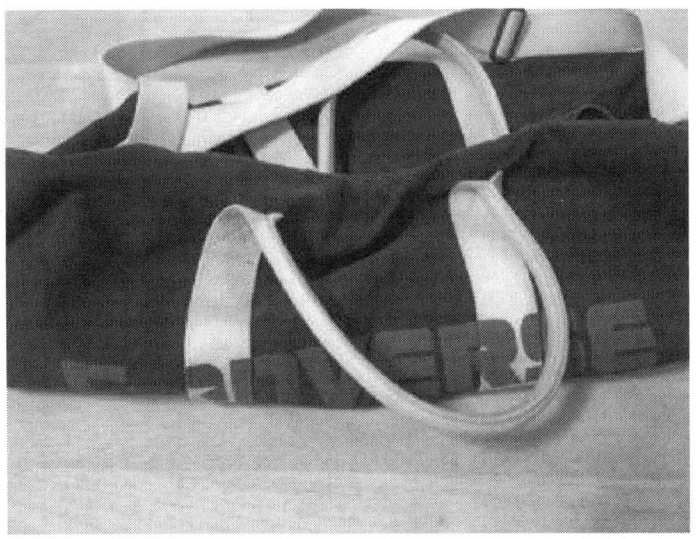

Clothing

I personally stay away from synthetic shirts, but if you don't mind the feel of synthetics I'd say go for it as synthetics will last longer. I still like to box in cotton workout t-shirts. Under Armour and Adidas are my favorite brands currently. Every couple months even the washer machine won't make them clean and they end up in the trash. I'd say definitely wear synthetic workout shorts with compression gear underneath or long compression leggings. Many boxers I've seen like to wear compression long sleeve shirts as well, but like I mentioned I can't stand the feel so I still stick with cotton shirts. To feel good while you workout that's the key.

Punching Combinations (Numbers)

Different gyms do things differently, different couches will have different punch combinations. At my first gym the punching combination 1, 2, 3, 4, 5, 6 for right hand boxers was a straight left or jab 1, right cross or right straight 2, left hook 3, left uppercut 4, right uppercut 5, and ended with a right hook at number 6. Most gyms I've seen differ from this approach. 1 is a left straight, 2 is a right cross or straight right, left hook 3, right hook 4, left uppercut 5, and right uppercut is 6. I think the later punch numbering system is more intuitive and I think that's why most boxing fitness classes teach boxing this way. If you are unsure of the punch numbers ask your instructor. You should be learning the punch numbers in class, if you aren't you probably aren't at a "real" boxing gym. As you're learning the punching combinations repeat the numbers to yourself everytime you throw a punch. Be mindful of the number combination in your head at all times.

Left Handed Or Right Handed?

When you first start out your coach will probably ask you if your left handed or right handed. If you are a right handed boxer you'll box in an orthodox stance with left hand and left foot in the lead and right foot behind you. If you are left handed you'll be boxing in the southpaw position where everything is reversed. The right hand and right foot will be forward and the left foot will be behind you. Now, there are no rules you absolutely have to box this way. A right handed boxer can box in the southpaw stance just as a left handed boxer can box in the orthodox stance. Most fitness boxing gyms I've been to lately usually switch between the two stances. The advantages and disadvantages to boxing stances usually come only if you are sparring. My recommendation is box the way you feel most comfortable, where you have the best form, or just do whatever your boxing coach tells you.

Good Technique

Remember good technique is key especially when boxing. Concentrate on throwing good punches with correct form and less about throwing as many punches as possible. I've noticed in some boxing fitness classes the goal is to throw as many punches as possible and as hard as you can without even a thought about form. Don't be like the people around you. They won't last long. Good technique is key to staying engaged, improving, and enjoying boxing long term.

Focus on getting power starting at your feet through the hips, torso, then out through your arms. Throwing a punch works the whole body. It's not about just your arm. Always concentrate on what the instructor is trying to teach, learn the fundamentals first, don't develop bad habits. You want to think long term, not compete with the person punching as fast as they can next to you.

The Basic Punches

Cover

Your hands should be protecting your face at all times, punches should always lead to your hands coming back to your face. This is your primary defense. Think of your arm as a piston in an engine, it always comes back to it's original starting position. To help with cover imagine that your holding two small mobile phones just below your ears. Your elbows should be down covering your body at the same time, close into your sides. Even if you don't plan on ever sparring it's a good habit to cover your face and let elbows extend down to your body at all times. Remember punches come at your face and body. Some of the most painful shots are body shots, as a beginner you'll want to just protect your face.

You'll quickly learn that sometimes the best fighters are chopped down from the trunk. At all times keep your chin tucked and eyes on your boxing opponent.

Jab

Every boxer needs a good jab. When throwing a jab don't just think of your arm throwing the punch, think of your entire body throwing out the punch and extending through your arm. Take a step forward with your left foot and throw your jab with left hand (Reversed for left handed boxers). Be sure to fully extend your arm starting from your face, turning your wrist, then retracting your arm back to your cover position. The jab sets up other punches or combinations of punches. The jab isn't meant to be a knockout power punch.

Right Cross

The right cross or right straight is your power punch. The jab sets up the combination and your right cross finishes it. To achieve this punch take a small step with your left foot (Reversed for lefties), you should then rotate your body and right (Pivot) foot in the direction of your right arm. Once again the power of this punch isn't in how fast your right arm moves towards your target. The power comes from your entire body from the ground up, twisting towards the target.

Left Hook, Right Hook

Raise your left hand out in front of you, palm down, or palm towards you. Just a quick note on hook styles, I used to throw left and right hooks with palm down. Once I switched to throwing hooks with my palm facing towards myself, think of stirring a thick pot of stew, my shoulders stopped hurting and I gained more power with my hook. I now always throw left and right hooks palm towards me, see what style works for you. If you are sparring or competing that's when you need to adjust styles. For fitness boxing it shouldn't matter. When throwing a left hook be sure to be pivoting your left leg. When throwing a right hook be sure to be pivoting your right leg. The power doesn't come from the arms, once again it comes from the entire body from the ground up. If you are using cheap gloves and cheap hand wraps and you start developing significant power you may start to feel your hands "tweaking" when throwing power hooks. I completely stopped this from happening after switching over to the Title Gel Bag Gloves. That's why it's so important to invest in good boxing equipment. You won't box long if you go with the cheap stuff.

Right Uppercut, Left Uppercut

The right and left uppercut can be devastating punches. Just look at old videos of Mike Tyson, I can't think of anyone that threw the uppercut more viciously than Tyson. Similar to the hooks when you throw a left uppercut pivot your front left foot. When throwing a right uppercut pivot your back right foot (Reversed for southpaw stance boxers). Also, be sure to have your knees bent slightly when throwing a uppercut. The power comes from the legs and body. The uppercut is for close range, there are no haymaker uppercuts. A good gym will have bags specifically designed for uppercuts, but I've noticed many fitness boxing gyms do not have uppercut bags. Be careful when throwing an uppercut on a standard heavy bag, I usually do not throw at full power because there is a chance punch won't land flush with the bag thus hurting your wrist.

Basic Defense

I won't go into defense as much as I did for punching. This book is written for boxing beginners and fitness boxers primarily, but it's good to know the basics none the less. My suggestion to learn the basics of defense as quickly as possible is to get a friend or gym partner to help. Throw punches very lightly and slowly at each other and see how the body naturally reacts. If someone is throwing a hook at the body, you'll want to drop your elbow down to protect your body. What if they then go back to the face with the other hand? Lessons are learned quickly because the stakes are real, you don't want to get hit. Don't forget to keep your hands up protecting your face even while another hand is coming at the body. It's one thing to talk about defense, but a whole different thing when you see an actual punch coming at you. Once again the drill should be slow and without any power, learn by practicing this way is ideal. If you can't practice this way I recommend at all times imagining the heavy bag is your opponent sometimes the puncher, sometimes the counter puncher. Keep your hands up at all times, protect your body, slip, duck, move around the bag, change angles, change punches, lean back, change levels, use the space, whatever you do don't stay in one spot. You're an easy target if you don't move.

Slipping

Slip on the most basic level is to move your head side to side to avoid the punches being thrown at you. Lets say a boxer throws a left jab at you, you'll want to slightly turn your left shoulder towards the right, dip your head slightly towards the right, and slightly crunch forward to the right. Reverse the movement if boxer throws a right towards you. A slip is something you have to see, I'd suggest asking your coach or watch videos on YouTube. It's very difficult to do well and actually avoid a punch being thrown at you.

Rolling

Next, you have the roll which you can use in conjunction with slipping. To roll you'll be ducking and rolling the torso left to right, right to left. Also called bob and weaving (See below).

Bobbing and Weaving

Bob and weaving is kind of like rolling. Basically you are doing a up and down "V" shape with your body movement. Bob and weaving is also called rolling (See previous).

Ducking

It's like it sounds bend your knees while keeping your eyes on your opponent. This is something you can use to get out of the way of a jab for example. Ducking is also called dipping.

Parrying

When you parry you are basically deflecting punches from coming at your face. You are catching your opponents punch and directing away. If you have a jab coming at you slap punch down with right hand. If you have a right hand coming at you slap down with left hand. The motion should be quick and don't forget defense or counter punching opportunities during and after movement.

Catching

With your gloves up to your face you catch the punch with both gloves.

Blocking

Blocking is where one catches incoming punches like a mitt palm facing forward.

Movement

Don't stay in one place while punching the heavy bag. In a real fight you'll need to move, use the space around you. If you can't move side-to-side lean back. If you get stuck in the corner of the ring move around your opponent as get out of corner or against the ropes. If you don't move around you are a really easy target. Even if you don't ever plan on sparring moving around the heavy bag is a good habit to get into.

Clinching

This is pretty much only applies to amateur and professional boxers, but late in the rounds when your arms and body are tired clinching is an effective technique for rest. Just grab on your opponent as long as you need rest or when the referee breaks up the clinch.

Scratching The Surface

I'm just scratching the surface when it comes to defensive techniques. There are many more ways to avoid and protect yourself from punches, but these are the basics and most widely taught. For most of my book audience who just wants to enjoy themselves in a boxing gym you only need to learn a few basic defensive techniques.

Preventing Possible Injuries

Like I mentioned earlier in this book I've been boxing more than 10 years and have had many chances of getting injured. Below are some ways to project your body and make sure you'll be boxing long term.

Protect Your Wrists

When I joined my first boxing gym I stupidly used the provided cheap and well used boxing gloves. DON'T DO THIS! I can't stress this enough, do not use the provided boxing gloves in your boxing fitness class. The gloves gyms provide are usually worse than crap. Go online and usually a $40 min. pair is way better than anything you'll get in your boxing fitness class. More on gloves I recommend later, but quickly I recommend getting the Title Bag Gloves which retail for about $100 - $130. When I first started boxing and throwing punches my wrists were hurting. That's because cheap gloves do not give you a lot of wrist support especially when you're throwing power hooks. If you want to box long term you will need to buy good bag gloves not sparring gloves (Unless you plan to spar), but good bag gloves (For hitting the heavy bag). Your wrists will thank you and they shouldn't hurt after this. During the past 10 plus years I've gone through 4 pairs of Title Boxing Gloves and 1 pair of RDX Gloves. The RDX hurt my wrists, they tweaked a bit when throwing hard hooks, so I went back to the Title Gel.

Recommended Gloves

Almost every web site that recommends gloves has the TITLE Gel World Bag Gloves on their list. The Title Gel Bag Gloves are my #1 go to boxing glove. I see at least one pair at any boxing gym I go to. Get them on Amazon at the time of this writing for $120. $120 is less than most gyms charge per month so it's really not that much money.

Trust me getting good gloves should be your number one priority. Good boxing gloves make boxing fun, you'll be able to focus on your boxing workout, not your hurting hands, wrists, and knuckles.

If you can't afford Title Gel Bag Gloves try out the RDX Cowhide Bag Gloves that retail for about $60 on Amazon. I'd recommend these gloves only for beginners because once you develop your power punch you'll need high quality bag gloves that protect your wrists like the Title Gel Boxing Gloves.

Bag Glove Recommendations

Here is a list of well-reviewed gloves. Like I've mentioned I've only tested the Title Gels and RDX Cow Hide Leather Gel Boxing Gloves, but Title Gel are consistently one of the most popular gloves at any gym I've been to and still one of my favorites. Other highly reviewed bag gloves include Ringside Gel Shock Boxing Super Bag Gloves, Title Gel Rush Bag Gloves, and Title Boxing Pro Heavy Bag Gloves.

Sparring Gloves

If you plan to spar you'll probably want a par of sparring gloves as well. If you aren't planning on sparring skip this section. Sparring gloves differ from bag gloves in that they are designed to have more padding up front to minimize the impact of the glove on your sparring partner. Bag gloves have denser padding that can last even when repeatedly hit against a heavy bag. I've used to use my bag gloves in sparring so it's not totally a necessity, but using sparring gloves will definitely be appreciated by your sparring partner. Many people recommend the Winning Gloves, but they are also some of the more expensive gloves out there. Good lower priced gloves include the Rival RS2V High Performance Sparring Gloves, Twins Special BGVL-3 Gloves, Cleto Reyes Training Gloves, Rival High Performance Hook-and-Loop Sparring Gloves and the Ringside IMF Tech are also recommended sparring gloves.

Sizing

For men I'd recommend the 16 oz. or large size gloves if they don't list ounces. For women I'd recommend the small or medium, something less than 16 oz. I'm 6 ft. and have always used a 16 oz. or "large" (Depends on web site how they categorize either 16 or large). The lighter the glove the easier it is to throw a punch, but the downside is less protection. It's ultimately up to you. I've even seen in the some boxing fitness classes people using MMA gloves which I definitely don't recommend. If you don't know what size to get just feel it out the first class or two. Use the boxing gloves provided by the gym or briefly borrow someone's gloves to see what weight feels best for you. You don't want your hand to feel like it's an anchor, but you also don't want a glove so small that it doesn't offer any padding or support.

Boxing Glove Tip

If you're concerned and money isn't an issue there are actual dryers that you can hang your sweaty boxing gloves on. If your like most people and money isn't limitless I recommend using Lysol Disinfectant Spray when you're done using your gloves. Stuffing your gloves with newspaper works as well to dry them out. After you take your sweaty hands out of your gloves and remove your hand wraps use a bit of hand sanitizer.

Knees

For me my knees started hurting first. To solve this problem I moved from tennis shoes to investing in wrestling shoes, then finally getting good boxing shoes, I also lost some weight. These simple things solved the problem.

Boxing as an Art Form

This just started for me in the past few years, but once you have your punches down and pretty much every move and combination is committed to memory boxing can become art. I'm just slightly overstating here, but at a certain skill level boxing becomes creative expression. It has become a way to express my feelings, creativity, style, in a way it's almost like dancing. When starting you may think a 1,2, 3 combo can be achieved in one way. After a while in the sport you can make a 1,2,3 your own. You can put your own stamp and style on it. There's an old saying that anyone can look good on a heavy bag, so don't get too confident. If you start sparring or moving on beyond that, you'll be quickly humbled, still doesn't take away from the point however. When you know enough you can make boxing your own.

The Importance Of Warming Up

Stretch

I can't stress how important it is for you to warm up first when boxing. If nothing else stretch, especially your arms and shoulders. One stretch I like that really gets the shoulders is put your arms above your head and lean them against the heavy bag. Push into the bag and let your arms go behind you. You should feel this in your shoulders. Stretching is number one. If your boxing fitness gym doesn't begin with a warm up I'd move onto another gym or quickly come up with a routine of your own.

Jump Rope

After or before you stretch jump rope for a minimum of 3 minutes. Jump rope builds coordination and stamina. I'm not sure if you can call yourself a real boxer if you don't know how to jump rope. Just start with the standard motion, but the combinations and patterns you can do with your jump rope are endless. I'd search YouTube or just Google jump rope patterns, but here are some of the routines I do (See below). I highly respect boxing gyms that add jump rope as part of the class warm up routine.

Jump Rope Tips

- Some possible patterns include standard flat footed jump rope. Try alternating with your elbows in, compact, close to your torso and out wide.

- Reverse jump rope direction and jump rope "backwards."

- Alternate hoping on left foot 2 times and right foot 2 times.

- Alternate hoping on one foot 10 times and the other 10 times.

- Alternate hoping on the left food 2 times, land on two feet, then right foot 2 times. Go back and forth with this pattern.

- Cross jump jump and jump once doing a "cross over" bring back to a normal jump rope pattern and repeat the "cross over" once you feel steady again.

- Do a cross over and continue jumping with your arms crossed, in the cross over position.

- Jump rope normally and every 2-4 jumps swing jump rope from side to side. Then go back to jumping normally and repeat swing.

- Double unders. Swing rope like normal, but instead of only swinging jump rope under you once this time you'll do two. Anyone into Cross-Fit will be familiar with double unders. I took a beginners Cross-Fit Class and in a group of about 10 I was the only one that could do double unders since I already had been doing them in boxing class.

- Swing your right leg front to back, then left leg front to back as you jump rope normally.

- Swing your right leg right from front, back, side to side and repeat with other leg.

- Do jumping jacks, in and out motion with your feet as you jump rope normally.

- Criss cross your legs as you jump rope normally.

- Do squats as you jump rope as normally as you can.

- Do twists as you jump rope normally. Move your torso from side to side. Or you can twist left jump, center jump, right jump, and repeat.

- Jump rope normally, but twist to one side.

- Do a boxing shuffle as you jump rope. Switch off between an orthodox stance (Right handed) or southpaw (Left handed).

- Jump rope with your feet together and hop back and forth.

- Jump rope with one foot up in the air and jump side to side, front to back. Repeat with other leg.

Speed Bag

Does your gym have a speed bag? If not, you may want to find another gym. Any self respecting boxing gym will have at least one speed bag station. Don't be afraid of the speed bag, go over to it and start hitting it. Start with the combination 1,2 .. 1,2 switching from right to left, left to right, repeating. Go on YouTube and search speed bag how to. I remember when I first started speed bag, I had been hitting the bag for about a year and couldn't put the speed into speed bag if you know what I mean. There's a certain beginner way people hit the bag 1,2 switch hands 1,2 it's slow, usually hit harder than needed, no consistency or beat. I had been hitting the speed bag this beginner way and then my gym closed for about two weeks during winter break and New Year's. I had no speed bag practice during this time, but when I came back and to my surprise my speed back had sped up tremendously. It was like night and day. My hands got quicker doing nothing other than taking time off on winter break, my hands had magically became much quicker. It's like my subconscious needed a break to commit the speed bag technique to memory.

If you practice and practice and no matter

what you do that speed bag doesn't speed up it may be the gyms equipment. I've noticed that even in good boxing gyms the quality of the speed bag varies greatly. Sometimes the speed bag isn't leather, sometimes it's not inflated, sometimes the speed bag swivel hardware is broken, many times the speed bag platform isn't robust enough and the vibrations cause the speed bag to slow down prematurely. It's funny the speed bag is the one piece of equipment you can probably judge the entire gym on. If the gym has a quality speed bag that works it's probably a exceptional boxing gym.

Speed Bag Starter Tip

When I first started on the speed bag I was slow. I couldn't believe how fast that thing was swinging. Now it's all about the pattern and the rhythm and I don't really need to even look at the bag. One drill that I was taught is hitting the bag with your eyes closed and focusing in on the rhythm rather than the actual bag. Once you learn the rhythm of the speed bag you know the position of the bag at all times. What really helped me at first was zeroing in on a focal point. I found looking at the top portion of the speed bag, the top of the rain drop shaped speed bag, helped me track the movement of the bag better. Play around with starring at different parts of the bag to find what works best for you. Top, bottom, does the bag have a logo to stare at? Etc.

Double End Bag

Does your gym have a double end bag? If so use it! There are few things that will build timing and quickness better than a double end bag. The goal is not to punch the double end bag as hard as you can it's to develop timing, quickness, and footwork. If your gym doesn't have one I'd recommend going to Title Boxing or Amazon or wherever and picking one up. If you don't know what a double end bag is, it's a small leather ball attached to bungee cords on each end. One end of the bungee should be connected to your ceiling and the bottom bungee and be secured to the floor with a heavy weight if installing at home.

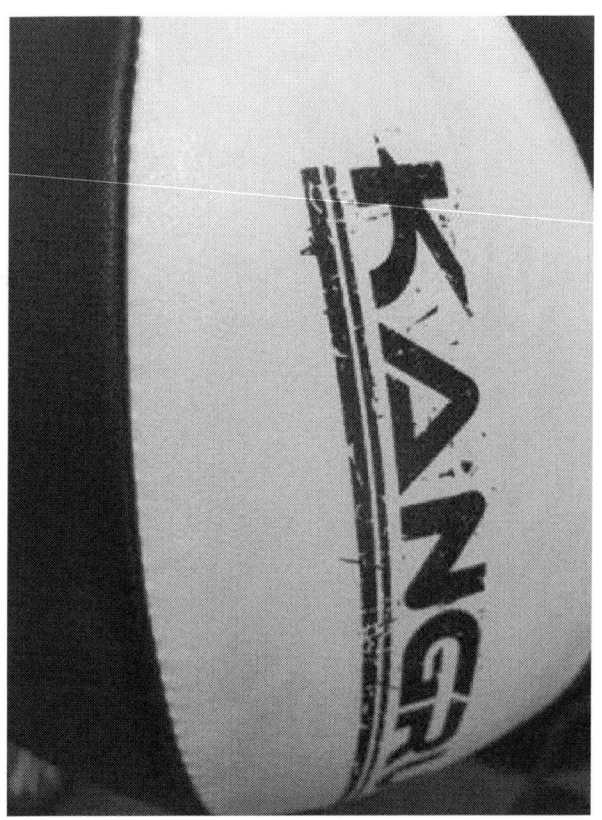

Slip Ball

This is kind of a fun product you can add to your home boxing gym. It's like heavy bag in that it hangs from your ceiling, but it's much smaller in size. The small bag swings back and forth and a boxer can practice basic slip, bob a weave, head movement, body movement techniques. This set up doesn't have to be fancy, you could even hang a tennis ball from a string.

Focus Mitts

Most fitness boxing gyms don't use focus mitts, but if yours does this is a definite plus. If your boxing gym lets students practice mitts with other students or trainers you are probably going to a more legit boxing gym. Focus mitts are a flat, padded target, the wearer of the mitts usually calls out combinations for the boxer to follow. The wearer of the mitt can also counter with soft "punches" for example throwing a hook to the body to get boxer to protect his torso. Keeps puncher on guard to keep hands up and protecting his head and torso at all times. There is probably nothing that makes you feel more like a boxer than mitt training. If you haven't done focus mitt training yet I'd suggest finding a gym that incorporates this into their regular workouts or getting an hour or so of personal training.

Focus Shield

Another related piece of boxing equipment to the focus pads are focus shields. Like focus mitts the holder calls out punches or just moves shield. Focus shields are usually round, padded, and have handles on each side. They are great for hook and uppercut training.

If Sparring

If you'd like to spar, my suggestion is not using an open face headgear. My experience with open face head gear is I ended up with a bloody nose 60% of the time. If you're like me and your nose bleeds easily why not pay a little bit more and get a full face head gear or even better get a "Face Saver" or "Full Face" style head gear that completely covers up the entire face leaving only your eyes open. Once I started using the face saver style head gear I could concentrate on my punching and defense again, not my bleeding nose. It was like discovering a golden unicorn. The difference in sparring experience enjoyment was night and day. The Everlast Face Saver Headgear I purchased was about $100 at the Everlast web site.

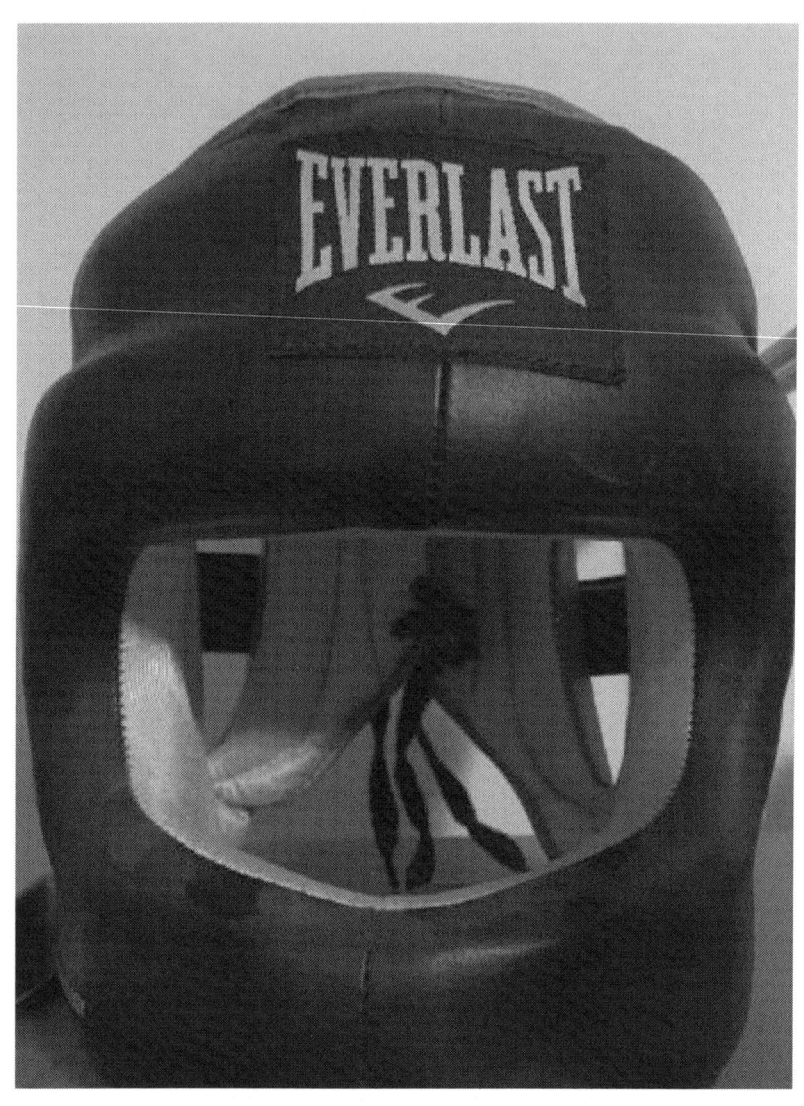

Mouth Guard

Don't forget your mouth guard when sparring and make sure it's one you mold it to your mouth/teeth first. Mouth guards can be priced anywhere from a few dollars all the way up to $100s for a custom mouth guard. According to NationwideChildrens.org a properly fitted custom mouth guard may reduce the rate of concussion as well as dental injuries. There are three types of mouth guards to consider from least expensive to most expensive. First is your standard ready-made or stock mouth guard, next the mouth-formed "boil and bite" mouth guard, and finally a custom-made mouthguard made by a dentist. One of the most important things for me when I was sparring was finding the right mouth guard that allowed for easy breathing. You don't want your boxing mouth guard to restrict the flow of air and you get winded that much faster. Some guards have built in holes to allow the boxing to breath such as the $34.99 Brain Pad 3XS Pro Super Gel Jaw-Joint Protector on the Title Boxing web site.

(Above) The mouth guard I used for sparring was the Everlast Ever-Guard. There are better newer versions of this mouth guard.

Concussions

There are few sports where the objective, least on the professional level of boxing, is to give your opponent a concussion or something close to that. I personally would advise against moving on from anything other than very light sparring with head gear. I think deciding whether or not your want to spare, become a amateur boxer, or move onto professional boxing is ultimately up to the individual. Boxing is a calling for many people, but make sure the trade off is worth the potential cost to your brain health. If you are an amateur or professional boxer, wait to go all out in the ring when it counts, in competition. Avoid proving yourself in gym sparring battles that have no purpose other than to satisfy one's ego. Before you start educate yourself, there is potential for concussions even when wearing head gear, don't fool yourself into thinking head gear makes boxing risk free. Make an informed decision after checking out all the educational resources dedicated to concussions and with eyes wide open make the decision that's right for you.

Don't Forget Other Forms Of Exercise

Don't forget other forms of working out such as running, lifting weights, ab work, and stretching like yoga. Just because you may be in the best shape of your life right now just after starting your new boxing class doesn't mean giving up on other forms of exercise completely. Don't forget that the gains won't last forever, you will hit a plateau at some point. I used to lift weights then started to box. After a while I noticed a lot of my muscle mass started to disappear. My shoulders started to hurt. I did get more flexible as the result of boxing and doing a aerobic workout, but there was a downside too. I solved a lot of my aches and pains by mixing in yoga 2-3 times a week and still practicing weight lifting at least once per week. Then the other 2 days I was boxing. When I was really starting to get sore I was boxing 3-5 times per week. That was too much for my body. To change things up I enjoy running 5Ks and obstacle course racing. I also started getting into not just boxing, but kickboxing as well. Kickboxing I feel adds a whole new dimension to the boxing experience. Boxing made me more coordinated in my feet and legs, but doing kickboxing for about two years now has brought the coordination to another level. I've also seen many of my boxing friends get into MMA classes or jiu jitsu classes.

What To Expect During Class

There should be some type of warm up, stretching, jump rope. You should hit the heavy bags, do some mitt work, speed bag, double end bag, medicine ball, weights, etc. If you are in a sparring class then you might mix in some sparring during these drills. Classes I've found usually end with an ab burnout session followed by light stretching. Every coach and class is different.

What To Look For In A Boxing Gym

I'm mostly talking about fitness boxing here, but I think having actual boxers as coaches is important. I believe if you have a boxer as a coach they are much more concerned with technique. I can't stress how important it is to learn good technique early on when you first start boxing. It all starts from this. Boxing is not seeing how many punches you can throw and how hard you throw them. There is so much more to boxing and a good coach will show you this.

ClassPass

I use app/web site called ClassPass. The gym I went to for 8 years I was a monthly subscriber, but after that I stared using a service called ClassPass (Except for one year period at the UFC Gym). ClassPass allows you to test out gyms without joining them. Also, I've used Groupon to test out a couple boxing gyms as well. My advice is to test boxing gyms before actually signing up with them. Each gym I've found has a distinct, unique culture. Some gyms are friendlier than others. Some gyms feel cliquish. Some gyms have better equipment than others. Most importantly find a boxing gym you like that makes you feel comfortable and welcomed. Boxing gym time should be fun and you should leave feeling good about yourself.

The Equipment

Find a gym with good equipment. You'll be happier, trust me. Go to a gym will genuine leather heavy bags, speed bag, weights, medicine balls, jump ropes, double end bag, mitts, focus shields, gloves and wraps for rent, and if possible find a gym with a boxing ring. Not that you will actually use the ring, but gyms with a ring are more likely to attract skilled boxers and skilled boxing couches. Don't be intimidated, even the most hardcore boxing gyms offer fitness classes. I for one at my old gym welcomed new students, frankly it gets boring seeing the same people in the gym day in day out. I'd say pretty much everybody wants and welcomes new students to the gym.

Location

To stick with your boxing fitness routine make sure the gym is relatively close to your house. I made the mistake of picking a gym that was downtown and I'm in the suburbs. The commute when I first started was a maximum of 30 min. each way, but then the tech. boom happened in my city and the commute that was just 30 min. became 45 min. average and up to 1 hour 30 min. at the worse in Friday rush hour. It was sad, but I had to find something closer. The upside of all the people moving into the region was that other boxing gyms started to pop up that were closer to me. Nothing could beat the gritty yet friendly boxing gym I went to for 8 years, but I finally found one closer. It's a close second to my original gym. Also, make sure there is parking next to the boxing gym. I remember trying a boxing gym downtown in my city and I not only had to search for parking I had to pay for it. I think it was $5 or something, but no one wants to pay a gym membership fee, drive, search for parking, and pay for it just to get a boxing workout in. My advice is make it fun. If the workout, gym culture, and overall commute don't make you feel happy you won't keep it up.

Home Boxing Gym

Don't have a boxing gym in your area? Although this is not ideal, you still can build a home boxing gym. I think working out with people and coaches teaches you things and pushes you more than being by yourself. First thing you'll need is a good heavy bag. I know you're tempted to go your local sporting goods store, but don't! Don't purchase cheap, crappy, utterly useless boxing equipment. Most of the cheap stuff found at local megastores is absolute garbage.

Heavy Bag For Home

Get a 100% leather hanging heavy bag, brands like Title or Ringside are a good option. If you don't want to hang a bag get a free standing bag. They will never be as good as a hanging bag, but they still can work decently. I use one by Century called the Wavemaster XXL Training Bag. Free standing bags will move around, even if they are full of water or stand so just keep that in mind. The Wavemaster is $300 on Amazon, but I purchased on Craigslist for $50. It's weird I've noticed used boxing equipment on Craigslist is worth almost nothing. Bargains are to be had on Craigslist. Shop Craigslist first before paying retail for your boxing equipment.

Double End Bag For Home

Get a double end bag for home. Make sure it's all leather and comes with an instillation kit. You will most likely end up attaching one end of the bungee rope to the ceiling and the other ends to weights on the floor. This is what I did for my garage double end bag setup.

Speed Bag For Home

Repeat after me.. "All speed bags are not created equal." When it comes to speed bags, they are awesome and absolutely a must in a home gym if you decide to go that route, but like heavy bags most are garbage. The speed bag needs to be leather and high quality, spend the extra money. The most important thing, however, is the platform that speed bag hangs on. There can be no vibration or that thing won't swing. The base needs to connect securely to the wall and the circular piece of wood that the leather speed bags hits needs to be heavy and substantial or it won't swing. If the bag doesn't swing it won't work, it won't be a speed bag, it will be a random hit, absorption, and come slowly back to you bag.

I've seen gyms put sandbags on top of their speed bag platforms, you may want to try this as a last resort.

Cheap Equipment Warning

There is nothing that upsets me more than cheap, garbage, boxing equipment. Most stuff you see, probably 95% at your local sports super center is absolute rubbish. Go to a boxing store, your boxing gym, Amazon (Purchase only well reviewed products), Title Boxing, Ringside, etc. Pay more! Do your research! Read reviews! Make phone calls! Talk to experts! Nothing will make you loose interest faster in boxing than using bad equipment.

Listen To Your Body

In boxing I think listening to your body is one of the most important things you can do. Boxing is something people get addicted to, something you love, that's why it's so easy to overtrain. Before you blow out your shoulder or knee listen to that pain. What is it saying? Most likely it's saying please, please, please, take a break. Or if you aren't that excited for your boxing class listen to that. You should be excited or your body is probably telling you need a break, slow down and let your muscles heal up before you start throwing punches again.

Common Sense Suggestions

- Drink lots of water
- Eat healthy, whole foods
- Eat protein, add protein shakes as needed
- Eat a balanced diet
- Eat fruits and vegetables
- Get enough sleep
- Nap when you need it
- Control stress (Though I've found you can channel frustration into energy well with boxing). Yoga and meditations helps.
- Take a multivitamin

Add to this list as needed, but these are just the common sense basics. You will notice more than other sports if you treated your body well the day before or not. Sometimes in the gym you'll be sluggish, but other times you'll surprise yourself and get a superhuman burst of energy. You can't fool yourself in boxing, what you do out of the gym translates directly to how well you perform in the gym.

Where Am I Now

I currently box 2 times a week, do hot yoga 2-3 times a week, and lift weights once per week. Occasionally I do Cross-Fit, 5K fun runs, and obstacle course racing. I mix regular boxing up with kickboxing. I find boxing is way better than weights for coordination, add kickboxing and this gets even more of your entire body involved. Yoga makes you leaner, improves flexibility, and helps reduce stress. Mix in other workouts as needed, all exercises should compliment one another.

Conclusion

At this point you should be excited about starting a boxing workout routine. Boxing truly is one of the best and most addictive workouts on Earth. It's not only physical, once you do it long enough it becomes a creative expression. When I'm boxing I sometimes feel everything making sense, it's my happy place, I could literally spend hours a day doing it if I had no responsibilities outside of the boxing gym.

You have the knowledge, but there's no change without action. Go out there and join a boxing gym today! If there is no boxing gym in your area start a club or build one in your garage or spare bedroom. Do whatever you need to do, just make it happen. Hopefully you'll be like me and develop a healthy addiction to the world's most addictive sport, boxing.

Dedication

I'd like to dedicate this book to all my past coaches. Thank you for all your support. Boxing has helped me get through many tough times in my life. When everything else was going wrong boxing remained one of the positive constants. Some days I'd come to the gym sick from stress and borderline depressed, but I never left boxing feeling worse than first arriving. It has not only got me through difficult times, it's also made me more resilient and confident in myself. Thank you coaches and thank you boxing!

Disclaimer

"This e-book is not intended to replace professional medical treatment. You should consult your physician or other health care professional before starting this or any other fitness program to determine if it is right for your needs. This book offers health, fitness and nutritional information and is designed for educational purposes only. You should not rely on this information as a substitute for, nor does it replace, professional medical advice, diagnosis, or treatment. Once again this e-book was developed by an individual and not a doctor/health/boxing professional. The information is based on the latest research and the author's personal experience."

Made in the USA
Middletown, DE
09 May 2019